I0625492

Gaslighting

A Survivor's Guide to Healing and Empowerment After Psychological Abuse

Cathleen R. Barton

Gaslighting: A Survivor's Guide to Healing and Empowerment After Psychological Abuse

Table of Contents

01: What is Gaslighting?

Gaslighting is a form of psychological manipulation in which a person or group seeks to sow seeds of doubt in a targeted individual or group, making them question their own memory, perception, or judgment. It is a tactic often used by abusers, dictators, and cult leaders to control and subjugate their victims. The term "gaslighting" comes from the 1938 stage play "Gas Light," in which a husband tries to drive his wife crazy by dimming the gas lights in their home and then denying that the light changed when his wife points it out.

There are several tactics that are commonly used in gaslighting. One is denial, in which the manipulator flatly denies that something happened or that they said something, even when there is clear evidence to the contrary. This can leave the victim feeling confused and uncertain, and they may begin to question their own recollection of events.

Another tactic is lying and exaggerating, in which the manipulator makes false or exaggerated claims about the victim or about events that have occurred. This can cause the victim to doubt their own perception of reality and to feel that they are unreliable or untrustworthy.

Manipulators may also use the tactic of withholding inform-ation, in which they selectively provide or withhold inform-ation in order to confuse and mislead the victim. This can make it difficult for the victim to understand what is hap-pening and can leave them feeling isolated and unsure of whom to trust.

A manipulator may also use the tactic of manipulating phys-ical evidence, such as altering documents or hiding objects, in order to support their claims and create confusion. This can leave the victim feeling uncertain and unsure of what is true.

One of the most insidious tactics of gaslighting is projection, in which the manipulator accuses the victim of the very things that they themselves are guilty of. For example, an abuser may accuse their victim of being manipulative or ab-usive, even though it is the abuser who is behaving that way. This can leave the victim feeling confused and unsure of their own actions, and can be especially effective in causing the victim to doubt their own judgment.

The effects of gaslighting can be devastating, as it can leave the victim feeling confused, isolated, and unsure of their own perceptions and judgment. It can also cause the victim to become more dependent on the manipulator, as they may come to rely on them for a sense of stability and guidance. In extreme cases, gaslighting can lead to the victim developing mental health problems such as anxiety, depression, and PTSD.

It is important to recognize the signs of gaslighting and to seek help if you or someone you know is being victimized in this way. Some common signs include feeling confused or unsure of what is happening, feeling isolated or cut off from support, and feeling like you are going crazy. If you suspect that you or someone you know is being gaslighted, it is important to seek help from a trusted friend, family member, or mental health professional. It is also important to remember that you are not alone and that there is support available.

It is important to remember that gaslighting is a form of abuse, and it is never the fault of the victim. The manipulator is solely responsible for their actions, and it is important to hold them accountable for their behavior.

01: WHAT IS GASLIGHTING?

If you are being gaslighted, it is important to try to maintain a sense of reality and to seek out supportive relationships with friends and family members who can help you to stay grounded and to feel confident in your own perceptions and judgment. It can be helpful to keep a journal or a record of events, as this can help you to better understand what is happening and can serve as evidence if you need to seek help or report the abuse.

It is also important to remember that you have the right to set boundaries and to assert your own needs and wants. This may be difficult if you are being gaslighted, as the manipulator may try to control your behavior and limit your autonomy. However, it is important to stand up for yourself and to assert your own rights and needs. This may involve seeking help from a therapist or counselor, or it may involve seeking support from friends and family members.

If you are in an abusive relationship and are being gaslighted, it may be necessary to leave the relationship in order to protect yourself and your well-being. This can be a difficult and frightening decision, but it is important to remember that you deserve to be treated with respect and to be in a healthy, safe relationship. There are resources available to help you leave an abusive relationship, such as domestic violence shelters and hotlines, and it is important to reach out for help if you need it.

In conclusion, gaslighting is a harmful and abusive tactic that is used to manipulate and control others. It can have serious effects on the victim's mental health and well-being, and it is important to recognize the signs of gaslighting and to seek help if you or someone you know is being victimized in this way. Remember that you are not alone, and that there is support available to help you heal and to regain control over your life.

It is also important to remember that gaslighting is not just something that happens in personal relationships. It can also occur in professional settings, such as the workplace or in political contexts.

In the workplace, a manager or colleague may use gaslighting tactics to undermine an employee's confidence and to make them question their own abilities or judgment. This can be especially harmful if the employee is isolated or lacks support from their colleagues.

In political contexts, gaslighting can be used as a tactic to manipulate public opinion and to spread misinformation. This can be especially dangerous, as it can erode trust in institutions and undermine the foundations of democracy.

It is important to be aware of the potential for gaslighting in all types of relationships and to be alert to the signs of manipulation. It is also important to support and empower those who may be victims of gaslighting, and to hold manipulators accountable for their actions.

It is worth noting that it is possible for someone to gaslight themselves, particularly if they have low self-esteem or a history of being manipulated or abused. In these cases, it can be helpful to seek therapy or counseling to work through these issues and to build a stronger sense of self-worth and self-confidence.

Overall, gaslighting is a harmful and insidious form of manipulation that can have serious consequences for the victim. It is important to be aware of the signs of gaslighting and to seek help if you or someone you know is being victimized in this way. Remember that you deserve to be treated with respect and to be in healthy, supportive relationships, and that there is help available to support you in

01: WHAT IS GASLIGHTING?

achieving this.

02: The Signs of Gaslighting

Gaslighting is a form of psychological manipulation that can be difficult to recognize, especially if you are in a close relationship with the manipulator. However, there are several signs that can indicate that you or someone you know is being gaslighted.

One of the most common signs of gaslighting is feeling confused or unsure of what is happening. The manipulator may deny or distort events, or may withhold information, in order to create confusion and uncertainty. As a result, the victim may feel like they are "going crazy" or like they can't trust their own perceptions.

Another sign of gaslighting is feeling isolated or cut off from support. The manipulator may try to isolate the victim from friends and family, or may try to undermine their relationships with others, in order to make them more reliant on the manipulator. This can leave the victim feeling alone and unsure of whom to trust.

A third sign of gaslighting is feeling like you are constantly second-guessing yourself or doubting your own judgment. The manipulator may try to undermine the victim's confidence in their own abilities or judgment, and may try to make them feel incompetent or incapable. This can leave the victim feeling insecure and unsure of themselves.

A fourth sign of gaslighting is experiencing a change in your personality or behavior. The manipulator may try to control the victim's behavior or to make them conform to their expectations, and this can lead to the victim changing their personality or behavior in order to please the manipulator.

A fifth sign of gaslighting is experiencing a change in your relationships with others. The manipulator may try to alienate the victim from their friends and family, or may try to manipulate the victim's relationships with others in order to further their own goals. This can leave the victim feeling isolated and alone.

It is worth noting that not all of these signs necessarily indicate that someone is being gaslighted. However, if you are experiencing several of these signs, or if you are feeling confused, uncertain, or isolated, it may be worth considering the possibility that you are being manipulated.

It is important to remember that if you are being gaslighted, it is not your fault. The manipulator is solely responsible for their behavior, and it is important to hold them accountable for their actions. If you are in an abusive relationship and are being gaslighted, it may be necessary to leave the relationship in order to protect yourself and your well-being.

There are resources available to help you leave an abusive relationship, such as domestic violence shelters and hotlines, and it is important to reach out for help if you need it.

If you suspect that you or someone you know is being gaslighted, it is important to seek help from a trusted friend, family member, or mental health professional. It is also important to remember that you are not alone and that there is support available to help you heal and to regain control over your life.

It can be especially difficult to recognize the signs of gaslighting if you are in a close relationship with the manipulator, as they may have gained your trust and may have convinced you that they have your best interests at heart. However, it is important to be aware of the potential for manipulation and to be alert to the signs that something may be wrong.

Some other signs of gaslighting to watch out for include:

– The manipulator consistently contradicts your perceptions or memories of events, even when you are sure you are right.

– The manipulator frequently changes the subject or distracts you when you try to discuss something that is important to you.

– The manipulator minimizes your feelings or concerns, or makes you feel like you are being oversensitive or unreasonable.

– The manipulator tries to make you feel guilty or ashamed for things that are not your fault.

– The manipulator tries to control your behavior or decisions, or makes you feel like you have to ask permission for things.

– The manipulator tries to turn others against you, or undermines your relationships with friends and family.

If you are experiencing these signs, it is important to take them seriously and to seek help if you need it. Remember that you have the right to be treated with respect and to be in healthy, supportive relationships, and that you deserve to feel safe and valued.

It is also important to be aware of the potential for gaslighting in professional or political contexts. In these settings, manipulators may use similar tactics to undermine your confidence, to spread misinformation, or to control public opinion. It is important to be aware of these tactics and to be vigilant against them.

Overall, the signs of gaslighting can be subtle and may not be immediately obvious. However, if you are experiencing confusion, uncertainty, or a sense that something is not right, it is important to trust your instincts and to seek help if you need it. Remember that you are not alone and that there is support available to help you heal and to regain control over your life.

It is also important to recognize that gaslighting is a form of abuse, and it is never the victim's fault. The manipulator is solely responsible for their actions, and it is important to hold them accountable for their behavior.

If you are in a relationship with someone who is gaslighting you, it can be difficult to know what to do. It is important to remember that you have the right to set boundaries and to assert your own needs and wants. This may involve setting limits on the time you spend with the manipulator or on the types of conversations you have with them. It may also involve seeking support from friends and family or from a therapist or counselor.

If you are in an abusive relationship and are being gaslighted, it may be necessary to leave the relationship in order to protect yourself and your well-being. This can be a difficult and frightening decision, but it is important to remember that you deserve to be treated with respect and to be in a healthy, safe relationship. There are resources available to help you leave an abusive relationship, such as domestic violence shelters and hotlines, and it is important to reach out for help if you need it.

It is also important to remember that it is possible to recover from gaslighting and to rebuild your sense of self-worth and self-confidence. This may involve seeking therapy or counseling, or it may involve building new, supportive relationships with friends and family. It is important to be patient with yourself and to give yourself time to heal.

In conclusion, gaslighting is a harmful and abusive tactic that can have serious consequences for the victim. It is important to recognize the signs of gaslighting and to seek help if you or someone you know is being victimized in this way. Remember that you are not alone, and that there is support available to help you heal and to regain control over your life.

03: The Impact of Gaslighting on Your Mental Health

Gaslighting is a form of psychological manipulation in which a person or group seeks to sow seeds of doubt in a targeted individual, making them question their own memory, perception, or judgment. Gaslighting can occur in personal relationships, at work, or in political or social groups. It is often a subtle form of abuse, as the manipulator may try to convince their victim that they are simply misunderstanding things or are overly sensitive. However, the effects of gaslighting can be severe and long-lasting, causing serious damage to a person's mental health and well-being.

One of the most insidious aspects of gaslighting is that it can be difficult to detect, especially if the manipulator is skilled at concealing their true intentions. They may deny saying or doing certain things, or present conflicting information in a way that leaves the victim feeling confused and uncertain. This can lead to the victim feeling isolated and disconnected from their own reality, as they struggle to make sense of what is happening around them.

The constant questioning of one's own perceptions and

memories can be emotionally and mentally exhausting, leading to feelings of anxiety, depression, and low self-esteem. The victim may also feel a sense of powerlessness and helplessness, as they are unable to control the manipulation or stop it from happening. In some cases, they may begin to doubt their own sanity, leading to serious mental health issues such as paranoia, dissociation, and even psychosis.

Gaslighting can also have a profound impact on a person's relationships and social interactions. The manipulator may try to alienate the victim from their friends and family, further isolating them and making it more difficult for them to seek support. The victim may also become more reliant on the manipulator for emotional support, leading to an unhealthy dynamic in which they are constantly seeking validation and approval from their abuser.

There are several ways in which a person can protect themselves from the effects of gaslighting. It is important to be aware of the signs of gaslighting and to trust one's own perceptions and instincts. It can also be helpful to seek support from trusted friends, family members, or a mental health professional. It is also important to set boundaries and to communicate openly and honestly with the manipulator, letting them know that their behavior is not acceptable.

In some cases, it may be necessary to seek help from a legal or social services agency in order to protect oneself from on-going abuse. It is also important to remember that no one deserves to be subjected to gaslighting or any other form of psychological abuse, and that it is never too late to seek help and make positive changes in one's life.

In conclusion, gaslighting is a serious form of psychological manipulation that can have a devastating impact on a person's mental health and well-being. It is important to be aware of the signs of gaslighting and to seek support in order to protect oneself from its harmful effects. With the right help and support, it is possible to break free from the cycle of abuse and to reclaim one's own sense of self and reality.

It is important to recognize that gaslighting is a form of abuse and that it can have serious consequences for a person's mental health. If you suspect that you or someone you know is being gaslighted, it is important to seek help and support.

03: THE IMPACT OF GASLIGHTING ON YOUR MENTAL HEALTH

There are several resources available for individuals who are experiencing gaslighting or other forms of abuse. These may include therapy or counseling, support groups, or legal or social services agencies. These resources can provide the necessary support and guidance to help individuals cope with the effects of gaslighting and to develop healthy coping strategies.

It is also important to remember that it is never too late to seek help and to make positive changes in one's life. No one deserves to be subjected to gaslighting or any other form of abuse, and it is possible to break free from the cycle of abuse and to reclaim one's own sense of self and reality.

It is important to recognize that gaslighting can have serious and long-lasting effects on a person's mental health and well-being. If you or someone you know is experiencing gaslighting or other forms of abuse, it is important to seek help and support as soon as possible. With the right resources and support, it is possible to break free from the cycle of abuse and to rebuild one's sense of self and reality.

It is important to recognize that gaslighting can be a subtle and insidious form of abuse, and that it can be difficult for a victim to identify and acknowledge what is happening to them. This can make it difficult for them to seek help and support, as they may not realize the full extent of the manipulation and abuse they are experiencing.

One of the most important things a victim of gaslighting can do is to seek support from trusted friends, family members, or a mental health professional. These individuals can provide a sense of grounding and help the victim to validate their own perceptions and experiences. It can also be helpful to seek out a support group or therapy, where the victim can connect with others who have experienced similar abuse and can learn healthy coping strategies.

It is also important for victims of gaslighting to set boundaries and to communicate openly and honestly with the manipulator. This can help to establish clear expectations and to assert control over the situation. In some cases, it may be necessary to seek help from a legal or social services agency in order to protect oneself from ongoing abuse.

It is also important to remember that it is never too late to seek help and to make positive changes in one's life. No one deserves to be subjected to gaslighting or any other form of abuse, and it is possible to break free from the cycle of abuse and to reclaim one's own sense of self and reality.

In conclusion, the impact of gaslighting on mental health can be severe and long-lasting. It is important to recognize the signs of gaslighting and to seek help and support in order to protect oneself from its harmful effects. With the right resources and support, it is possible to break free from the cycle of abuse and to rebuild one's sense of self and reality.

04: The Cycle of Gaslighting and How to Break Free

The cycle of gaslighting is a pattern of manipulation and abuse that can be difficult for a victim to recognize and break free from. Gaslighting is a form of psychological manipulation in which a person or group seeks to sow seeds of doubt in a targeted individual, making them question their own memory, perception, or judgment. Gaslighting can occur in personal relationships, at work, or in political or social groups. It is often a subtle form of abuse, as the manipulator may try to convince their victim that they are simply misunderstanding things or are overly sensitive.

The cycle of gaslighting typically begins with the manipulator planting seeds of doubt in the victim's mind. This may involve denying saying or doing certain things, or presenting conflicting information in a way that leaves the victim feeling confused and uncertain. The manipulator may also try to alienate the victim from their friends and family, making it more difficult for them to seek support or validation from others.

As the cycle continues, the victim may begin to doubt their own perceptions and memories, leading to feelings of anxiety, depression, and low self-esteem. They may also feel a sense of powerlessness and helplessness, as they are unable to control the manipulation or stop it from happening. In some cases, they may even begin to doubt their own sanity, leading to serious mental health issues such as paranoia, dissociation, and psychosis.

The cycle of gaslighting can be difficult to break, as the manipulator may be skilled at concealing their true intentions and at making the victim feel like they are the problem. However, there are steps that a victim of gaslighting can take to break free from this cycle and to reclaim their sense of self and reality.

One of the most important things a victim of gaslighting can do is to seek support from trusted friends, family members, or a mental health professional. These individuals can provide a sense of grounding and help the victim to validate their own perceptions and experiences. It can also be helpful to seek out a support group or therapy, where the victim can connect with others who have experienced similar abuse and can learn healthy coping strategies.

It is also important for victims of gaslighting to set boundaries and to communicate openly and honestly with the manipulator. This can help to establish clear expectations and to assert control over the situation. In some cases, it may be necessary to seek help from a legal or social services agency in order to protect oneself from ongoing abuse.

It is also important for victims of gaslighting to practice self-care and to engage in activities that promote their own well-being. This may include exercising, engaging in hobbies, or seeking out activities that bring them joy and fulfillment. Taking care of oneself can help to build resilience and to provide a sense of stability and purpose, which can be especially important during times of uncertainty and stress.

Breaking free from the cycle of gaslighting can be a challenging and difficult process, but it is possible with the right support and resources. It is important to remember that no one deserves to be subjected to gaslighting or any other form of abuse, and that it is never too late to seek help and make positive changes in one's life. By seeking support and learning healthy coping strategies, victims of gaslighting can break free from the cycle of abuse and reclaim their sense of self and reality.

It is also important for victims of gaslighting to be aware of the signs of gaslighting and to trust their own perceptions and instincts. This can help them to recognize when they are being manipulated and to seek help and support before the cycle of abuse becomes more entrenched. Some common signs of gaslighting may include:

– Denial of events or actions: The manipulator may deny saying or doing certain things, even when confronted with evidence to the contrary.

– Presenting conflicting information: The manipulator may present conflicting information in a way that leaves the victim feeling confused and uncertain.

– Isolating the victim: The manipulator may try to alienate the victim from their friends and family, making it more difficult for them to seek support or validation from others.

– Diminishing the victim's accomplishments: The manipulator may attempt to belittle or diminish the victim's accomplishments in order to make them feel incompetent or unworthy.

– Blaming the victim: The manipulator may attempt to shift blame onto the victim, making them feel responsible for the manipulator's behavior.

It is important for victims of gaslighting to be aware of these signs and to trust their own perceptions and instincts. If you suspect that you or someone you know is being gaslighted, it is important to seek help and support as soon as possible. With the right resources and support, it is possible to break free from the cycle of abuse and to reclaim your sense of self and reality.

In conclusion, the cycle of gaslighting is a pattern of manipulation and abuse that can have serious and long-lasting effects on a person's mental health and well-being. It is important to be aware of the signs of gaslighting and to seek help and support in order to break free from this cycle. With the right resources and support, it is possible to break free from the cycle of abuse and to reclaim your sense of self and reality. So, it is very important to recognize the signs of gaslighting and take necessary actions to break free from it.

It is also important for individuals who have experienced gaslighting to be mindful of their own mental health and to

seek help if needed. The effects of gaslighting can be severe
and long-lasting, and it is important to address any mental
health issues that may arise as a result of the abuse. This
may include seeking therapy or counseling, joining a support group, or seeking help from a mental health professional.

It is also important for individuals who have experienced
gaslighting to practice self-care and to engage in activities
that promote their own well-being. This may include exercising, engaging in hobbies, or seeking out activities that
bring them joy and fulfillment. Taking care of oneself can
help to build resilience and to provide a sense of stability
and purpose, which can be especially important during
times of uncertainty and stress.

It is also important for individuals who have experienced
gaslighting to be mindful of their relationships and to surround themselves with supportive and caring individuals.
This may involve seeking out new friendships or building
healthier relationships with existing friends and family
members. It may also be necessary to set boundaries with
individuals who are not supportive or who engage in manip-

ulative or abusive behaviors.

Breaking free from the cycle of gaslighting can be a difficult and challenging process, but it is possible with the right support and resources. It is important to remember that no one deserves to be subjected to gaslighting or any other form of abuse, and that it is never too late to seek help and make positive changes in one's life. By seeking support and learning healthy coping strategies, individuals who have experienced gaslighting can break free from the cycle of abuse and reclaim their sense of self and reality.

05: The Role of Boundaries in Healing from Gaslighting

Boundaries are an important aspect of healthy relationships and can play a crucial role in the healing process for individuals who have experienced gaslighting or other forms of abuse. Gaslighting is a form of psychological manipulation in which a person or group seeks to sow seeds of doubt in a targeted individual, making them question their own memory, perception, or judgment. Gaslighting can occur in personal relationships, at work, or in political or social groups. It is often a subtle form of abuse, as the manipulator may try to convince their victim that they are simply misunderstanding things or are overly sensitive.

One of the most harmful effects of gaslighting is that it can leave victims feeling isolated and disconnected from their own reality. They may feel confused and uncertain about what is happening around them, and may struggle to trust their own perceptions and instincts. Setting boundaries is an important part of the healing process, as it helps individuals to reclaim their own sense of self and to assert control over their lives.

There are several types of boundaries that can be helpful for individuals who are healing from gaslighting. Physical boundaries involve setting limits on physical touch and proximity, and may include things like respecting personal space or setting rules about when and how physical contact is acceptable. Emotional boundaries involve setting limits on how much of one's own emotions and personal information are shared with others, and may include things like setting limits on how much emotional support is given or received. Mental boundaries involve setting limits on what information and ideas one is willing to accept or consider, and may include things like setting limits on how much time is spent engaging in certain activities or with certain people.

Setting boundaries can be a challenging process, especially for individuals who have experienced gaslighting or other forms of abuse. It may be difficult to assert control over one's own life and to set limits with manipulators or abusers. However, it is important to remember that setting boundaries is an important part of the healing process, and that it is possible to learn healthy ways of interacting with others.

There are several ways in which individuals can set and enforce boundaries in their relationships. One of the most effective ways is to communicate openly and honestly with others about what is and is not acceptable. This may involve setting clear limits and expectations, and being firm and assertive when these limits are crossed. It is also important to be consistent in enforcing boundaries, and to follow through with any consequences that may be necessary if boundaries are not respected.

Another important aspect of setting boundaries is learning to say "no" when necessary. This may involve setting limits on how much time or energy is given to others, or saying "no" to requests or demands that are not in one's own best interests. It is important to remember that it is okay to prioritize one's own needs and to set limits on how much time and energy is given to others.

It is also important for individuals who are healing from gaslighting to seek support from trusted friends, family members, or a mental health professional. These individuals can provide a sense of grounding and can help individuals to validate their own perceptions and experiences. It can also be helpful to seek out a support group or therapy, where individuals can connect with others who have experienced similar abuse and can learn healthy coping strategies.

In conclusion, boundaries play an important role in the healing process for individuals who have experienced gaslighting or other forms of abuse. Setting and enforcing boundaries can help individuals to reclaim their own sense of self and to assert control over their lives. It is important to communicate openly and honestly with others, to be consistent in enforcing boundaries, and to seek support from trusted individuals in order to learn healthy ways of interacting with others.

It is important for individuals who are healing from gaslighting to be mindful of their own mental health and to seek help if needed. The effects of gaslighting can be severe and long-lasting, and it is important to address any mental health issues that may arise as a result of the abuse. This may include seeking therapy or counseling, joining a support group, or seeking help from a mental health professional.

It is also important for individuals who are healing from gaslighting to practice self-care and to engage in activities that promote their own well-being. This may include exercising, engaging in hobbies, or seeking out activities that bring them joy and fulfillment. Taking care of oneself can help to build resilience and to provide a sense of stability and purpose, which can be especially important during times of uncertainty and stress.

It is also important for individuals who are healing from gaslighting to be mindful of their relationships and to surround themselves with supportive and caring individuals. This may involve seeking out new friendships or building healthier relationships with existing friends and family members. It may also be necessary to set boundaries with individuals who are not supportive or who engage in manipulative or abusive behaviors.

Healing from gaslighting can be a challenging and difficult process, but it is possible with the right support and resources. It is important to remember that no one deserves to be subjected to gaslighting or any other form of abuse, and that it is never too late to seek help and make positive changes in one's life. By seeking support and learning healthy coping strategies, individuals who have experienced gaslighting can break free from the cycle of abuse and re-claim their sense of self and reality.

It is also important for individuals who are healing from gaslighting to be aware of the potential triggers that may cause them to feel vulnerable or uncertain. Triggers may include certain people, places, or situations that remind the individual of the abuse they experienced. By being aware of these triggers, individuals can take steps to protect themselves and to maintain their own sense of stability and well-being.

One way to cope with triggers is to develop a plan for how to respond when they occur. This may involve seeking support from trusted friends or family members, practicing self-care activities, or seeking out a safe and supportive environment. It may also be helpful to talk through the trigger with a therapist or counselor, in order to better understand and manage the feelings that are associated with it.

It is also important for individuals who are healing from gaslighting to work on rebuilding their sense of self and trust in their own perceptions and instincts. This may involve seeking therapy or counseling, joining a support group, or engaging in activities that promote self-awareness and self-esteem. It is also important to remember that healing is a process and that it is okay to take things one step at a time.

In conclusion, healing from gaslighting is a process that requires time, patience, and support. By setting boundaries, seeking support, practicing self-care, and being aware of triggers, individuals who have experienced gaslighting can work towards rebuilding their sense of self and trust in their own perceptions and instincts. It is important to remember that no one deserves to be subjected to gaslighting or any other form of abuse, and that it is never too late to seek help and make positive changes in one's life.

06: The Importance of a Support System

Having a support system is an important aspect of mental health and well-being, and can be especially crucial for individuals who have experienced trauma or abuse. A support system can provide a sense of connection and belonging, and can offer emotional, practical, and social support. It can help individuals to feel less isolated and alone, and can provide a sense of hope and resilience during difficult times.

There are many different types of support systems, and what works best for one person may not be the same for another. Some people may find support through friends and family, while others may find it through professional support networks such as therapy or counseling. It is important for individuals to identify what types of support work best for them, and to build a support system that meets their needs.

One of the most important aspects of a support system is the ability to provide emotional support. This may involve listening to and validating an individual's experiences, offering words of encouragement or comfort, or simply being present for them during difficult times. Emotional support can help individuals to feel less alone and to cope with difficult emotions, and can be an important factor in helping them to heal and move forward.

Practical support can also be an important aspect of a support system. This may involve providing assistance with tasks such as grocery shopping or running errands, or offering financial or other resources. Practical support can help individuals to feel more secure and less overwhelmed, and can make a significant difference in their daily lives.

Social support is another important aspect of a support system. This may involve engaging in activities or hobbies with friends or family, or simply spending time together in a supportive and caring environment. Social support can help individuals to feel less isolated and more connected to others, and can provide a sense of meaning and purpose.

Having a support system is not always easy, and it may take time and effort to build a network of supportive relationships.

There are several steps that individuals can take to build a support system:

06: THE IMPORTANCE OF A SUPPORT SYSTEM

– Identify what types of support are most important to you: This may include emotional, practical, or social support, or a combination of all three. It is important to be honest with yourself about what you need and to seek out support that meets those needs.

– Reach out to others: It can be intimidating to ask for help, but it is important to remember that most people are willing to offer support if asked. Reach out to friends, family, or professionals and let them know what you need. It may also be helpful to join a support group or to seek out other resources such as therapy or counseling.

– Be open and honest: In order to receive support, it is important to be open and honest about your needs and feelings. This may involve sharing your experiences, talking about your emotions, or simply expressing a need for support. By being open and honest, you can build deeper and more meaningful relationships with others.

– Be willing to accept and give support: Support is a two-way street, and it is important to be willing to both give and receive support. This may involve offering practical or emotional support to others, or simply being present and available when needed. It is also important to be willing to accept support when it is offered, and to be open to trying new things or seeking help when needed.

– Take care of yourself: Building a support system is an important aspect of self-care, but it is not the only aspect. It is important to engage in activities that promote your own well-being, such as exercising, eating a healthy diet, and getting enough sleep. By taking care of yourself, you can build resilience and be better equipped to handle challenges and setbacks.

In conclusion, having a support system is an important aspect of mental health and well-being. It can provide a sense of connection and belonging, and can offer emotional, practical, and social support. There are many different types of support systems, and it is important for individuals to identify what works best for them and to build a support system that meets their needs. By reaching out to others, being open and honest, being willing to give and receive support, and taking care of themselves, individuals can build a strong and supportive network of relationships.

It is important to remember that building a support system

is a process, and that it may take time and effort to develop meaningful relationships. It is also important to be patient with yourself and to recognize that it is okay to take things one step at a time. Building a support system is not always easy, and it may involve facing challenges or setbacks along the way. However, with patience and persistence, it is possible to build a strong and supportive network of relationships that can provide a sense of connection, belonging, and hope during difficult times.

It is also important to be mindful of your own needs and boundaries when building a support system. It is okay to set limits on what you are willing and able to give, and to prioritize your own well-being. It is also important to be aware of any patterns of unhealthy or manipulative behavior in your relationships, and to set boundaries with individuals who are not supportive or who engage in abusive or manipulative behaviors.

Finally, it is important to remember that it is okay to seek help if you are struggling to build a support system or to cope with difficult emotions or experiences. Seeking help from a mental health professional or joining a support group can be an important step in the healing process, and can provide valuable resources and support.

In conclusion, the importance of a support system cannot be overstated. It can provide a sense of connection and belonging, and can offer emotional, practical, and social support. Building a support system is a process that may take time and effort, but with patience and persistence, it is possible to develop meaningful and supportive relationships. It is also important to be mindful of your own needs and boundaries, and to seek help if needed. By building a strong and supportive network of relationships, individuals can find hope and resilience during difficult times.

07: The Role of Counseling in Healing from Psychological Abuse

Counseling can be an important tool for individuals who are seeking to heal from psychological abuse. Psychological abuse, also known as emotional abuse or mental abuse, is a pattern of behavior that seeks to undermine an individual's sense of self-worth and confidence. It can involve things like manipulation, coercion, blame, criticism, or isolation, and can have serious and long-lasting effects on an individual's mental health and well-being.

Counseling can provide a safe and supportive environment for individuals to explore their experiences and emotions, and to work through the impact of abuse on their lives. It can also provide a space for individuals to learn healthy coping strategies and to develop a stronger sense of self and self-worth.

There are several ways in which counseling can be helpful for individuals who are healing from psychological abuse:

– Providing a safe and supportive environment: Counseling provides a space where individuals can feel safe and supported as they explore their experiences and emotions. This can be especially important for individuals who have experienced abuse, as it can help to build a sense of trust and openness that is necessary for healing.

– Validating experiences and emotions: Counseling can provide a space for individuals to have their experiences and emotions validated. This can be especially important for individuals who have experienced abuse, as they may feel that their feelings and perspectives are not being respected or understood. Validating an individual's experiences and emotions can help to build a sense of trust and can be an important step in the healing process.

– Exploring coping strategies: Counseling can provide a space for individuals to explore different coping strategies and to find what works best for them. This may involve learning new skills such as stress management or communication, or finding healthy ways to manage difficult emotions. Counseling can help individuals to develop a toolkit of coping strategies that they can draw upon in times of stress or hardship.

– Building self-worth and confidence: Counseling can help individuals to rebuild their sense of self-worth and confidence, which can be particularly important for those who have experienced abuse. Counseling can provide a space for individuals to work through any negative beliefs or self-doubt that may have been instilled by the abuser, and to develop a stronger sense of self and self-worth.

– Providing support and guidance: Counseling can provide ongoing support and guidance as individuals navigate the healing process. This can be especially helpful for individuals who are struggling to cope with the aftermath of abuse, and may feel overwhelmed or uncertain about what to do next. Counseling can provide a sense of direction and can help individuals to feel less alone and isolated as they work towards healing and recovery.

There are several different types of counseling that may be helpful for individuals who are healing from psychological abuse. Some common approaches include cognitive-behavioral therapy (CBT), dialectical behavior therapy (DBT), and trauma-focused therapy. These approaches may involve learning new coping strategies, exploring one's thoughts and feelings, or working through traumatic experiences in a safe and supportive environment. It is important for individuals to find a therapist who is trained in working with individuals who have experienced abuse, and who is able to provide the support and guidance that is needed.

It is important to remember that healing from psychological abuse is a process, and that it may take time and effort. Counseling can be an important tool in this process, and can provide a safe and supportive environment for individuals to explore their experiences and emotions, and to develop healthy coping strategies. By seeking counseling and support, individuals can work towards healing and recovery, and can build a stronger sense of self and self-worth.

It is also important for individuals who are seeking counseling to be patient with themselves and to recognize that healing is a process that may involve setbacks and challenges. It is important to be kind to oneself and to take things one step at a time. It is also important to be open to trying new things and to seeking additional support if needed.

It is also important for individuals who are seeking counseling to be aware of their own needs and boundaries, and to communicate these to their therapist. This may involve setting limits on the types of topics that are discussed, or setting boundaries around the amount of time and energy that is given to the therapy process. It is important to remember that it is okay to prioritize one's own well-being and to set limits when needed.

In conclusion, counseling can be an important tool for individuals who are seeking to heal from psychological abuse. It can provide a safe and supportive environment for individuals to explore their experiences and emotions, and to develop healthy coping strategies. By seeking counseling and support, individuals can work towards healing and recovery, and can build a stronger sense of self and self-worth. It is important to be patient with oneself, to be open to trying new things, and to be aware of one's own needs and boundaries in the therapy process.

08: The Process of Empowerment After Gaslighting

Empowerment is the process of regaining control over one's own life and well-being, and can be an important step in the healing process after experiencing gaslighting. Gaslighting is a form of psychological abuse that involves manipulating an individual's sense of reality, often in order to exert control over them. It can involve things like denying events or experiences, manipulating information, or causing the individual to doubt their own perceptions and memories. Gaslighting can have serious and long-lasting effects on an individual's mental health and well-being, and can make it difficult for them to trust their own thoughts and feelings.

The process of empowerment after gaslighting involves reclaiming one's own sense of self and reality, and rebuilding a sense of trust in oneself and one's own perceptions. It may involve seeking out support and resources, setting boundaries, and developing healthy coping strategies. Empowerment is a process that may take time and effort, but with patience and persistence, it is possible to regain control over one's own life and to move forward in a positive direction.

There are several steps that individuals can take to begin

08: THE PROCESS OF EMPOWERMENT AFTER GAS-LIGHTING

the process of empowerment after experiencing gaslighting:

– Seek out support and resources: It is important for individuals who are healing from gaslighting to seek out support and resources that can help them to rebuild their sense of self and trust in their own perceptions. This may involve seeking therapy or counseling, joining a support group, or seeking help from a trusted friend or family member.

– Set boundaries: Setting boundaries is an important aspect of empowerment after experiencing gaslighting. This may involve setting limits on the types of interactions or behaviors that are acceptable, or setting limits on the amount of time and energy that is given to certain relationships or activities. Setting boundaries can help individuals to protect their own well-being and to feel more in control of their own lives.

– Develop healthy coping strategies: Developing healthy coping strategies can be an important step in the process of empowerment after gaslighting. This may involve learning new skills such as stress management or communication, or finding healthy ways to manage difficult emotions. It may also involve finding activities or hobbies that bring joy and fulfillment, and that help to build a sense of purpose and meaning.

– Rebuild trust in oneself: Rebuilding trust in oneself can be a challenging but important aspect of the empowerment process after experiencing gaslighting. This may involve challenging negative beliefs or self-doubt that may have been instilled by the abuser, and rebuilding a sense of self-worth and confidence. It may also involve finding ways to validate one's own experiences and emotions, and to trust in one's own perceptions and instincts.

Empowerment after gaslighting is a process that may involve challenges and setbacks, but with patience and persistence, it is possible to reclaim control over one's own life and to move forward in a positive direction. It is important to be kind to oneself and to recognize that healing is a process that may take time. By seeking out support and resources, setting boundaries, developing healthy coping strategies, and rebuilding trust in oneself, individuals can work towards empowerment and recovery after experiencing gaslighting.

It is also important for individuals who are working towards empowerment after gaslighting to be mindful of their own needs and boundaries, and to prioritize their own well-being. This may involve taking breaks or setting limits on certain activities or relationships, or seeking additional support if needed. It is important to remember that it is okay to put one's own needs first and to prioritize self-care.

It is also important to be aware of any potential triggers that may arise during the empowerment process. Triggers are things that may remind an individual of the abuse they experienced, and can cause them to feel vulnerable or uncertain. By being aware of these triggers, individuals can take steps to protect themselves and to maintain their own sense of stability and well-being.

In conclusion, the process of empowerment after gaslighting involves reclaiming control over one's own life and well-being, and rebuilding a sense of trust in oneself and one's own perceptions. It may involve seeking out support and resources, setting boundaries, and developing healthy coping strategies. Empowerment is a process that may take time and effort, but with patience and persistence, it is possible to move forward in a positive direction. It is important to be mindful of one's own needs and boundaries, and to be aware of any potential triggers that may arise during the empowerment process. By taking these steps, individuals can work towards empowerment and recovery after experiencing gaslighting.

It is important to remember that the process of empowerment after gaslighting is unique to each individual, and what works for one person may not be the same for another. It is important for individuals to be patient with themselves and to recognize that healing is a process that may involve setbacks and challenges. It is also important to be open to trying new things and to seeking additional support if needed.

It is also important to be aware of any patterns of unhealthy or abusive behavior in one's relationships, and to set boundaries with individuals who are not supportive or who engage in abusive or manipulative behaviors. This may involve seeking therapy or counseling, or seeking help from a trusted friend or family member. By setting boundaries and seeking support, individuals can work towards building healthy and supportive relationships that are based on respect and trust.

It is also important for individuals who are working towards empowerment after gaslighting to be mindful of their own self-care and well-being. This may involve engaging in activities that promote physical and emotional health, such as exercising, eating a healthy diet, and getting enough sleep. By taking care of oneself, individuals can build resilience and be better equipped to handle challenges and setbacks.

In conclusion, the process of empowerment after gaslighting is a unique and individualized process that involves reclaiming control over one's own life and well-being, and rebuilding a sense of trust in oneself and one's own perceptions. It may involve seeking out support and resources, setting boundaries, and developing healthy coping strategies. By being patient with oneself, open to trying new things, and mindful of one's own self-care and well-being, individuals can work towards empowerment and recovery after experiencing gaslighting.

09: Rediscovering Your Worth and Building Self-Esteem

Rediscovering one's worth and building self-esteem are important steps in the process of personal growth and development. Self-esteem is defined as an individual's overall sense of self-worth and confidence, and is an important aspect of mental health and well-being. When we have healthy self-esteem, we are more likely to feel confident and capable, and to take risks and pursue our goals. When our self-esteem is low, we may feel uncertain or unworthy, and may struggle to take care of ourselves or to set healthy boundaries.

Rediscovering one's worth and building self-esteem can be a challenging but rewarding process, and may involve exploring one's own values, setting goals, and learning new skills. It is important to be patient with oneself and to recognize that building self-esteem is a process that may take time and effort.

There are several steps that individuals can take to rediscover their worth and build self-esteem:

– Explore your values: One of the first steps in rediscovering your worth and building self-esteem is to explore your own values and beliefs. This may involve asking yourself questions such as "What is important to me?", "What are my goals and aspirations?", and "What makes me feel fulfilled and satisfied?" By exploring your own values, you can begin to understand what is most important to you and to build a sense of purpose and direction in your life.

– Set goals: Setting goals is an important aspect of building self-esteem, as it provides a sense of direction and helps to focus our energy and efforts. Goals can be short-term or long-term, and can be related to various areas of our lives such as career, relationships, personal growth, or health and wellness. By setting goals and working towards their achievement, we can build a sense of accomplishment and self-worth.

– Learn new skills: Learning new skills is a great way to build self-esteem and to feel more confident and capable. This may involve learning a new hobby or skill, or pursuing education or training in a particular area. By challenging ourselves and expanding our knowledge and abilities, we can build self-esteem and feel more confident in our own abilities.

– Practice self-care: Taking care of ourselves is an important aspect of building self-esteem, as it helps us to feel more capable and in control of our lives. Self-care can involve things like exercising, eating a healthy diet, getting enough sleep, and taking time for relaxation and leisure. By taking care of ourselves, we can build resilience and feel more capable of handling challenges and setbacks.

– Seek support and resources: Seeking support and resources can be an important aspect of building self-esteem, especially if we are struggling with low self-esteem or self-doubt. This may involve seeking therapy or counseling, joining a support group, or seeking help from a trusted friend or family member. By seeking support and resources, we can gain valuable perspective and guidance, and can build a stronger sense of self-worth and confidence.

– Set boundaries: Setting boundaries is an important aspect of building self-esteem, as it helps us to protect our own well-being and to feel more in control of our lives. Boundaries can be physical, emotional, or mental, and may involve setting limits on the types of interactions or behaviors that are acceptable, or setting limits on the amount of time and energy that is given to certain relationships or activities. By setting boundaries, we can feel more in control of our own lives and more able to take care of ourselves.

– Practice gratitude: Practicing gratitude is a simple but powerful way to build self-esteem and to feel more positive and hopeful. This may involve keeping a gratitude journal or making a list of things that we are thankful for each day. By focusing on the things that are going well in our lives, we can build a sense of appreciation and positivity, and can feel more confident and capable.

– Seek positive role models: Seeking positive role models can be a helpful way to build self-esteem and to gain perspective on what is possible. This may involve finding individuals who inspire us or who have achieved success in areas that are important to us. By seeking positive role models, we can gain insight and inspiration, and can feel more motivated and capable of achieving our own goals.

In conclusion, rediscovering one's worth and building self-esteem are important steps in the process of personal growth and development. It is a process that may take time and effort, and may involve exploring one's values, setting goals, learning new skills, practicing self-care, seeking support and resources, setting boundaries, practicing gratitude, and seeking positive role models. By taking these steps, individuals can build a stronger sense of self-worth and confidence, and can feel more capable and in control of their own lives.

It is important to remember that building self-esteem is a process that may involve challenges and setbacks, and it is important to be patient with oneself and to recognize that it is a journey. It is also important to be kind to oneself and to recognize that we are all human and that it is okay to make mistakes. By practicing self-compassion and by focusing on our strengths and accomplishments, we can build self-esteem and feel more positive and confident.

It is also important to be aware of negative self-talk and to challenge negative beliefs or thoughts that may be hindering our self-esteem. Negative self-talk can be damaging to our self-esteem and can hold us back from achieving our goals. By recognizing and challenging negative self-talk, we can build a stronger sense of self-worth and confidence.

09: REDISCOVERING YOUR WORTH AND BUILDING SELF-ESTEEM

It is also important to be open to seeking support and resources if needed. This may involve seeking therapy or counseling, joining a support group, or seeking help from a trusted friend or family member. By seeking support, we can gain valuable perspective and guidance, and can build a stronger sense of self-worth and confidence.

In conclusion, building self-esteem is a process that involves exploring one's values, setting goals, learning new skills, practicing self-care, seeking support and resources, setting boundaries, practicing gratitude, and seeking positive role models. It is a process that may involve challenges and setbacks, and it is important to be patient with oneself and to recognize that it is a journey. By being kind to oneself, recognizing and challenging negative self-talk, and seeking support and resources if needed, individuals can build self-esteem and feel more positive and confident.

10: The Role of Self-Care in the Healing Process

Self-care is an important aspect of the healing process, and involves taking care of one's own physical, emotional, and mental well-being. It is a necessary and vital aspect of self-care that can help individuals to feel more balanced, grounded, and resilient. When we practice self-care, we are better equipped to cope with the challenges and stresses of life, and to make positive choices for ourselves.

There are many different forms of self-care, and what works for one person may not be the same for another. Some common forms of self-care include:

Exercise and physical activity: Exercise and physical activity are important forms of self-care that can help to reduce stress, improve sleep, and boost mood. This may involve engaging in activities such as walking, running, swimming, or yoga.

Eating a healthy diet: A healthy diet is an important aspect of self-care, as it can help to support physical and mental well-being. This may involve incorporating a variety of nutrients and whole foods into one's diet, and avoiding processed or unhealthy foods.

Getting enough sleep: Sleep is an important form of self-care, as it is essential for physical and mental health. It is important to aim for 7-9 hours of sleep each night, and to create a sleep-friendly environment that is conducive to rest.

Taking breaks and relaxation: Taking breaks and relaxation are important forms of self-care that can help to reduce stress and improve well-being. This may involve activities such as reading, watching a movie, or taking a relaxing bath.

Seeking social support: Social support is an important form of self-care, as it can help to reduce feelings of isolation and loneliness, and can provide a sense of connection and belonging. This may involve seeking out supportive friends and family members, or joining a support group.

Practicing mindfulness: Mindfulness is a form of self-care that involves bringing one's attention to the present moment, and can help to reduce stress and improve well-being. This may involve activities such as meditation, deep breathing, or journaling.

By incorporating self-care activities into our lives, we can support our own healing and well-being, and feel more balanced and resilient. It is important to recognize that self-care is a necessary and vital aspect of our overall well-

being, and to prioritize it in our daily lives. It is also important to remember that self-care is not selfish, but rather it is an essential aspect of taking care of ourselves and being able to give back to others.

Self-care is particularly important during the healing process, as it can help to reduce stress and improve well-being. When we are healing from a difficult or traumatic experience, it is common to feel overwhelmed, exhausted, or drained. Self-care can help to nourish and restore us, and can provide a sense of comfort and support. It can also help to reduce feelings of anxiety or depression, and can improve our overall sense of well-being.

There are several steps that individuals can take to prioritize self-care during the healing process:

10: THE ROLE OF SELF-CARE IN THE HEALING PROCESS

— Identify your needs: The first step in prioritizing self-care during the healing process is to identify your own needs and what forms of self-care are most helpful for you. This may involve exploring your own values and what brings you joy and fulfillment, or seeking guidance from a therapist or other trusted resource.

— Set boundaries: Setting boundaries is an important aspect of self-care, as it helps to protect our own well-being and to feel more in control of our lives. Boundaries can be physical, emotional, or mental, and may involve setting limits on the types of interactions or behaviors that are acceptable, or setting limits on the amount of time and energy that is given to certain relationships or activities. By setting boundaries, we can feel more in control of our own lives and more able to take care of ourselves.

— Make self-care a priority: Once you have identified your needs and set boundaries, it is important to make self-care a priority in your daily life. This may involve setting aside dedicated time for self-care activities, or incorporating self-care into your daily routine. It is also important to be mindful of your own self-care needs and to prioritize them in your daily life.

– Seek support: Seeking support is an important aspect of self-care, and can be especially helpful during the healing process. This may involve seeking therapy or counseling, joining a support group, or seeking help from a trusted friend or family member. By seeking support, we can gain valuable perspective and guidance, and can feel more connected and less alone.

In conclusion, self-care is an important aspect of the healing process, and involves taking care of one's own physical, emotional, and mental well-being. By incorporating self-care activities into our lives, we can support our own healing and well-being, and feel more balanced and resilient. It is important to prioritize self-care, set boundaries, and seek support during the healing process. By taking these steps, individuals can further support their healing journey and improve their overall sense of well-being.

It is important to recognize that self-care looks different for everyone, and what works for one person may not be the same for another. It is important to be mindful of your own needs and to experiment with different forms of self-care to see what works best for you. It is also important to be kind to yourself and to recognize that it is okay to take breaks and to set limits when needed.

It is also important to be aware of any patterns of unhealthy or self-defeating behavior, and to seek help if needed. This may involve seeking therapy or counseling, or seeking help from a trusted friend or family member. By seeking help and support, individuals can work towards building healthy and supportive relationships that are based on respect and trust.

In conclusion, self-care is an important aspect of the healing process, and involves taking care of one's own physical, emotional, and mental well-being. It is a necessary and vital aspect of self-care that can help individuals to feel more balanced, grounded, and resilient. By incorporating self-care activities into our lives, setting boundaries, and seeking support, individuals can further support their healing journey and improve their overall sense of well-being.

11: Navigating Life After Gaslighting: Tips for Moving Forward

Navigating life after gaslighting can be a challenging and difficult process, as it involves rebuilding trust in oneself and one's own perceptions, and reclaiming control over one's own life and well-being. It is a process that may take time and effort, but with patience and persistence, it is possible to move forward in a positive direction.

There are several steps that individuals can take to navigate life after gaslighting and to move forward:

– Seek support: Seeking support is an important aspect of navigating life after gaslighting, as it can provide a sense of connection and belonging, and can help to reduce feelings of isolation and loneliness. This may involve seeking therapy or counseling, joining a support group, or seeking help from a trusted friend or family member. By seeking support, individuals can gain valuable perspective and guidance, and can feel more connected and less alone.

– Set boundaries: Setting boundaries is an important aspect of navigating life after gaslighting, as it helps to protect one's own well-being and to feel more in control of one's own life. Boundaries can be physical, emotional, or mental, and may involve setting limits on the types of interactions or behaviors that are acceptable, or setting limits on the amount of time and energy that is given to certain relationships or activities. By setting boundaries, individuals can feel more in control of their own lives and more able to take care of themselves.

– Practice self-care: Practicing self-care is an important aspect of navigating life after gaslighting, as it helps to reduce stress and improve well-being. Self-care can involve activities such as exercise, eating a healthy diet, getting enough sleep, and taking time for relaxation and leisure. By taking care of oneself, individuals can build resilience and feel more capable of handling challenges and setbacks.

– Learn to trust oneself: Trusting oneself is an important aspect of navigating life after gaslighting, as it involves rebuilding trust in one's own perceptions and experiences. This may involve learning to recognize and challenge negative self-talk, and working to develop a sense of self-acceptance and self-compassion. It is important to be patient with oneself and to recognize that rebuilding trust in oneself is a process that may take time.

– Seek out positive influences: Seeking out positive influences is an important aspect of navigating life after gaslighting, as it can help to provide a sense of support and encouragement. This may involve seeking out positive role models or seeking out supportive friends and family members. By seeking out positive influences, individuals can gain insight and inspiration, and can feel more motivated and supported.

– Set goals: Setting goals is an important aspect of navigating life after gaslighting, as it provides a sense of direction and helps to focus energy and efforts. Goals can be short-term or long-term, and can be related to various areas of one's life such as career, relationships, personal growth, or health and wellness. By setting goals and working towards their achievement, individuals can build a sense of accomplishment and self-worth.

In conclusion, navigating life after gaslighting can be a challenging and difficult process, but with patience and persistence, it is possible to move forward in a positive direction. By seeking support, setting boundaries, practicing self-care, learning to trust oneself, seeking out positive influences, and setting goals, individuals can navigate life after gaslighting and work towards rebuilding trust in oneself and reclaiming control over one's own life and well-being.

It is important to recognize that navigating life after gaslighting is a process that may involve challenges and setbacks, and it is important to be patient with oneself and to recognize that it is a journey. It is also important to be kind to oneself and to recognize that we are all human and that it is okay to make mistakes. By practicing self-compassion and by focusing on our strengths and accomplishments, we can build self-esteem and feel more positive and confident.

It is also important to be aware of negative self-talk and to challenge negative beliefs or thoughts that may be hindering our progress. Negative self-talk can be damaging to our self-esteem and can hold us back from achieving our goals. By recognizing and challenging negative self-talk, we can build a stronger sense of self-worth and confidence.

It is also important to be open to seeking support and resources if needed. This may involve seeking therapy or counseling, joining a support group, or seeking help from a trusted friend or family member. By seeking support, we can gain valuable perspective and guidance, and can build a stronger sense of self-worth and confidence.

In conclusion, navigating life after gaslighting is a process that involves seeking support, setting boundaries, practicing self-care, learning to trust oneself, seeking out positive influences, and setting goals. It is a process that may involve challenges and setbacks, and it is important to be patient with oneself and to recognize that it is a journey. By being kind to oneself, recognizing and challenging negative self-talk, and seeking support and resources if needed, individuals can navigate life after gaslighting and work towards rebuilding trust in oneself and reclaiming control over one's own life and well-being.

12: The Importance of Self-Compassion in Healing from Psychological Abuse

Self-compassion is an important aspect of healing from psychological abuse, as it involves treating oneself with kindness, understanding, and care, and recognizing that we are all human and that we all make mistakes. It is a powerful tool that can help individuals to heal from psychological abuse and to build a stronger sense of self-worth and confidence.

Self-compassion involves three core components: self-kindness, common humanity, and mindfulness.

– Self-kindness involves treating oneself with kindness and understanding, rather than with judgment or criticism. It involves being gentle and caring towards oneself, and recognizing that we all have flaws and limitations.

– Common humanity involves recognizing that suffering and struggles are a common part of the human experience, and that we are not alone in our experiences. It involves recognizing that we are all connected and that we all experience difficult emotions and challenges.

12: THE IMPORTANCE OF SELF-COMPASSION IN HEALING FROM PSYCHOLOGICAL ABUSE

– Mindfulness involves bringing awareness to the present moment and to our own thoughts and emotions without judgment. It involves accepting our experiences and emotions as they are, rather than trying to avoid or suppress them.

Self-compassion can be a powerful tool in healing from psychological abuse, as it helps to reduce feelings of shame and self-blame, and can help individuals to feel more accepting and understanding towards themselves. It can also help to reduce feelings of anxiety and depression, and can improve overall well-being.

There are several ways that individuals can practice self-compassion:

– Practice self-kindness: This may involve speaking to oneself in a kind and caring manner, or engaging in activities that bring joy and fulfillment.

– Remember that we are all human: This may involve reminding oneself that it is okay to make mistakes, and that we all have flaws and limitations.

12: THE IMPORTANCE OF SELF-COMPASSION IN HEALING FROM PSYCHOLOGICAL ABUSE

– Practice mindfulness: This may involve activities such as meditation, deep breathing, or journaling.

– Seek support: This may involve seeking therapy or counseling, joining a support group, or seeking help from a trusted friend or family member.

By practicing self-compassion, individuals can build a stronger sense of self-worth and confidence, and can feel more accepting and understanding towards themselves. It is an important aspect of healing from psychological abuse, and can help individuals to feel more resilient and capable of coping with challenges and setbacks.

It is important to recognize that practicing self-compassion is a process that may involve challenges and setbacks, and it is important to be patient with oneself and to recognize that it is a journey. It is also important to be kind to oneself and to recognize that we are all human and that it is okay to make mistakes. By focusing on our strengths and accomplishments, and by seeking support and resources if needed, we can build self-compassion and feel more positive and confident.

12: THE IMPORTANCE OF SELF-COMPASSION IN HEALING FROM PSYCHOLOGICAL ABUSE

In conclusion, self-compassion is an important aspect of healing from psychological abuse, and involves treating oneself with kindness, understanding, and care, and recognizing that we are all human and that we all make mistakes. It is a powerful tool that can help individuals to heal from psychological abuse and to build a stronger sense of self-worth and confidence. By practicing self-compassion, individuals can feel more accepting and understanding towards themselves, and can build resilience and feel more capable of coping with challenges and setbacks.

It is important to recognize that healing from psychological abuse is a process that may involve challenges and setbacks, and it is important to be patient with oneself and to recognize that it is a journey. It is also important to be kind to oneself and to recognize that it is okay to take breaks and to set limits when needed. By practicing self-compassion and by seeking support and resources if needed, individuals can further support their healing journey and build resilience and well-being.

It is also important to be aware of any patterns of unhealthy or self-defeating behavior, and to seek help if needed. This may involve seeking therapy or counseling, or seeking help from a trusted friend or family member. By seeking help and support, individuals can work towards building healthy and supportive relationships that are based on respect and trust.

In conclusion, healing from psychological abuse is a process that involves practicing self-compassion, seeking support, and being aware of any patterns of unhealthy or self-defeating behavior. It is a process that may involve challenges and setbacks, and it is important to be patient with oneself and to recognize that it is a journey. By being kind to oneself, seeking support and resources if needed, and working towards building healthy and supportive relationships, individuals can further support their healing journey and build resilience and well-being.

13: Finding Hope and Resilience After Gaslighting

Finding hope and resilience after gaslighting can be a challenging and difficult process, as it involves rebuilding trust in oneself and one's own perceptions, and reclaiming control over one's own life and well-being. It is a process that may take time and effort, but with patience and persistence, it is possible to find hope and resilience and to move forward in a positive direction.

There are several steps that individuals can take to find hope and resilience after gaslighting:

– Seek support: Seeking support is an important aspect of finding hope and resilience after gaslighting, as it can provide a sense of connection and belonging, and can help to reduce feelings of isolation and loneliness. This may involve seeking therapy or counseling, joining a support group, or seeking help from a trusted friend or family member. By seeking support, individuals can gain valuable perspective and guidance, and can feel more connected and less alone.

– Set boundaries: Setting boundaries is an important aspect

of finding hope and resilience after gaslighting, as it helps to protect one's own well-being and to feel more in control of one's own life. Boundaries can be physical, emotional, or mental, and may involve setting limits on the types of interactions or behaviors that are acceptable, or setting limits on the amount of time and energy that is given to certain relationships or activities. By setting boundaries, individuals can feel more in control of their own lives and more able to take care of themselves.

– Practice self-care: Practicing self-care is an important aspect of finding hope and resilience after gaslighting, as it helps to reduce stress and improve well-being. Self-care can involve activities such as exercise, eating a healthy diet, getting enough sleep, and taking time for relaxation and leisure. By taking care of oneself, individuals can build resilience and feel more capable of handling challenges and setbacks.

– Learn to trust oneself: Trusting oneself is an important aspect of finding hope and resilience after gaslighting, as it involves rebuilding trust in one's own perceptions and experiences. This may involve learning to recognize and challenge negative self-talk, and working to develop a sense of self-acceptance and self-compassion. It is important to be patient with oneself and to recognize that rebuilding trust in oneself is a process that may take time.

– Seek out positive influences: Seeking out positive influences is an important aspect of finding hope and resilience after gaslighting, as it can help to provide a sense of support and encouragement. This may involve seeking out positive role models or seeking out supportive friends and family members. By seeking out positive influences, individuals can gain insight and inspiration, and can feel more motivated and supported.

In conclusion, finding hope and resilience after gaslighting is a process that involves seeking support, setting boundaries, practicing self-care, learning to trust oneself, and seeking out positive influences. It is a process that may involve challenges and setbacks, and it is important to be patient with oneself and to recognize that it is a journey. By taking these steps, individuals can find hope and resilience after gaslighting and work towards rebuilding trust in oneself and reclaiming control over one's own life and well-being.

13: FINDING HOPE AND RESILIENCE AFTER GAS-LIGHTING

It is important to recognize that finding hope and resilience after gaslighting is a process that may involve challenges and setbacks, and it is important to be patient with oneself and to recognize that it is a journey. It is also important to be kind to oneself and to recognize that we are all human and that it is okay to make mistakes. By focusing on our strengths and accomplishments, and by seeking support and resources if needed, we can build hope and resilience and feel more positive and confident.

It is also important to be aware of negative self-talk and to challenge negative beliefs or thoughts that may be hindering our progress. Negative self-talk can be damaging to our self-esteem and can hold us back from achieving our goals. By recognizing and challenging negative self-talk, we can build a stronger sense of hope and resilience.

It is also important to be open to seeking support and resources if needed. This may involve seeking therapy or counseling, joining a support group, or seeking help from a trusted friend or family member. By seeking support, we can gain valuable perspective and guidance, and can build a stronger sense of hope and resilience.

13: FINDING HOPE AND RESILIENCE AFTER GAS-LIGHTING

In conclusion, finding hope and resilience after gaslighting is a process that involves seeking support, setting boundaries, practicing self-care, learning to trust oneself, and seeking out positive influences. It is a process that may involve challenges and setbacks, and it is important to be patient with oneself and to recognize that it is a journey. By being kind to oneself, recognizing and challenging negative self-talk, and seeking support and resources if needed, individuals can find hope and resilience after gaslighting and work towards rebuilding trust in oneself and reclaiming control over one's own life and well-being.

One way to find hope and resilience after gaslighting is to focus on small steps and progress, rather than on the overall journey. This can help to break the process down into manageable chunks, and can help to provide a sense of accomplishment and progress. It is important to be patient with oneself and to recognize that healing is a process that may take time, and to celebrate small victories along the way.

It is also important to remember that it is okay to feel a range of emotions, including anger, sadness, and frustration, and to allow oneself to feel and process these emotions. By acknowledging and expressing these emotions, individuals can begin to heal and move forward.

It is also important to be mindful of self-care and to prioritize taking care of oneself. This may involve activities such as exercise, eating a healthy diet, getting enough sleep, and taking time for relaxation and leisure. By taking care of oneself, individuals can build resilience and feel more capable of handling challenges and setbacks.

In conclusion, finding hope and resilience after gaslighting is a process that involves seeking support, setting boundaries, practicing self-care, learning to trust oneself, and seeking out positive influences. It is a process that may involve challenges and setbacks, and it is important to be patient with oneself and to recognize that it is a journey. By focusing on small steps and progress, allowing oneself to feel and process a range of emotions, and prioritizing self-care, individuals can find hope and resilience after gaslighting and work towards rebuilding trust in oneself and reclaiming control over one's own life and well-being.

Thank You

As we reach the end of this book, I want to say thanks for reading this book.

I want to get this information out to as many people as possible. If you found this book helpful, I would greatly appreciate you leaving me a review. This helps others find the book as well.

Disclaimer

This document is geared towards providing exact and reliable information in regards to the topic and issue covered. The publication is sold on the idea that the publisher is not required to render an accounting, officially permitted, or otherwise, qualified services. If advice is necessary, legal, financial, medical or professional, a practiced individual in the profession should be ordered.

This information is not presented by a financial or medical practitioner and is for entertainment, educational and informational purposes only. The content is not intended as a substitute for professional medical advice, diagnosis, or treatment. Always seek the advice of your physician or other qualified health care provider with any questions you may have regarding a medical condition. Never disregard professional medical advice or delay in seeking it because of something you have read.

The information provided herein is stated to be truthful and consistent, in that any liability, in terms of inattention or otherwise, by any usage or abuse of any policies, processes, or directions contained within is the solitary and utter responsibility of the recipient reader. Under no circumstances

DISCLAIMER

will any legal responsibility or blame be held against the publisher for any reparation, damages, or monetary loss due to the information herein, either directly or indirectly.